compass.

poems by

Angela Brown

Finishing Line Press
Georgetown, Kentucky

compass.

ACKNOWLEDGMENTS

I would like to give a heartfelt thanks to the amazing people of Finishing
Line Press for taking a chance on me and my unruly little poems.

Publisher: Leah Huete de Maines
Editor: Christen Kincaid
Cover Art: ©2012-2024 Angie Brown Artistry, LLC
Author Photo: ©2012-2024 Angie Brown Artistry, LLC
Cover Design: Elizabeth Maines McCleavy

Order online: www.finishinglinepress.com
            also available on amazon.com

Author inquiries and mail orders:
Finishing Line Press
PO Box 1626
Georgetown, Kentucky 40324
USA

Contents

"Perhaps all the dragons in our lives are princesses who are only waiting to see us act, just once, with beauty and courage."

Rainer Maria Rilke, *Letters to a Young Poet*

the scarecrow dressed in lace flees from herself.

Every day I lay upon these tracks at dawn
and pray
for a train to come
and crush every bone in my body,
to crack my skull in two-
            anything to be free of you.
            I'd do anything to be free of you.
At dusk (if I'm still breathing),
my lungs will be
empty, weeping stones,
my breath
burnt offerings of poetry.

Everything is on the ground.
Everything is scrambling in the dirt to an unknown heir.
The soil is rich here-
            a fine place to be miscarried.
                This is a fine place to be miscarried:
                    dried flowers & bones for the grave of the buried.

every image is.

Some nights she sleeps in the soil,
rises to praise the sun.
Some nights she hangs upside down
hair falling toward the ground,
her tears tear flowers in two-
        pouring hard till she drowns.

She crushes me with words like a blade of grass at her heel,
breath as wind whipping through weeds.
I am an image standing still,
        begging for The Artist to notice me.

But she…

tall standing tree,
unknown breed
growing at nature's edge,
from a single seed-

        a fearless blossom at risk.

She is a precipice.

No vase can hold her.

am I good enough for you?

Will you write me this *one*—chance meeting of our lips before I
    disappear?

Will you write me into the tomb of your gaze,
bury me inside your leatherbound book
where your pen presses down
so hard?
Will you carve your prayer into my tender belly,
til your ink and my blood
become one?

Alone in our dark poem,
your aching core crushes me,
with fists of iron and nickel.
Your steel milk melts inside of me
and I can no longer tell where your waist ends and mine begins.

I would pour out every drop of myself to please you.
I would bleed out every last metaphor for you to swallow my art
    whole,
to seize my gift and twist it to fit your every ambition.

I could live inside your secret diary,
in the shadowy creases of your parchment.
I would die for you to write for me,
to be the tragic and beautiful ghost that forever haunts your story.

reminiscence.

We all have our own vines to pull,
snakes to make smile,
bones to bury.

I thought I had made it-
        when I fully disappeared.
But the mirror never dies.
With truth told in lies,
old wounds become immortalized
in portraits.

I am not alive.

I am still-life.

last incarnation.

I no longer know when we are.
your gravity decides
our future, locked in rings,

                    otherworldly things.

Beneath you, stars seem close.

The curve of my back is closer
as you pull me in.

Light spills,
and spreads

filling space
with no sound.

Silence is a name in itself.

We're on the ground now.
You've brought the rings down

into flesh and bone.

Push me deep into this earth.
One last incarnation,
and we'll be home.

days in the afternoon.

Feeding things,
things that feed.
Sentinels and sharp objects.
The lazy river that took us everywhere
and nowhere.

The showdown.
The burning things.
The potions we made,
buried
and died.

I love you like blood knows itself
and cells divide.

I love you...

as only love can hide.

relative.

The light show
spectacular.
Homemade lasers
and radio
transmissions
from far away-

                                    come close.

Sky full of stars,
fatherless as they are.
           How alone am I?

Spinning nowhere
and never known.

You taught me The Theory of Everything,
The Big Bang,
how the universe is expanding
and my youth contracts and folds in on itself.

I am 40 now.

Never seems forever...

and the stars don't love me.

ellipses...

And there was never a bookend between us.
Our story stretched through every chapter,
every revision, every tear,
to be continued...
to be continued...
to be continued...
Every ellipses kept us holding,
and holding,
and holding on moments,
minutes.
Days of waiting
and writing,
waiting
and wanting.
I have written of you for ages,
the black and white
consonants and vowels of you.

My fingers surrender to the figure of you
forming out of fiction.
Your legacy left ink splatters,
dark fingerprints, everywhere your tale has touched me.

You touch me,
and metaphors explode from my mouth.
I feel my page turning
again,
again
and again.
Pen still warm,
waiting to be pushed
deeper
and thicker into this plot of you and I
forming,
with no title to contain us,
and every tumultuous tomorrow

to create
us.

parable

The page is cold
and curls away.

There is nowhere to share my sadness.

You are leaving
and I long for the places we have never spoken.

I find myself plagiarizing your stone hands
that never touched me.

Will you meet me in a far off death?
Pray with me
a new parable,
smoke signals,
a scent in the doorway?

I find myself
fixing a tale
of how to disappear into a place where you ever loved me,
or carve out this infinite ache-
                    heart-shaped,
                    the size of your palm.

Tears tuck me in
until then.

I have become a storyteller
telling the stories of men.

(full) fill me with love.

A moment with you is like
midnight dew
pressing
the unfolding petals of my rose.

A dream of you is like
stars posing madly
in the sky.
A million constellations dance wildly
before
my eyes.

What is this love
like
twin doves
dive deep to pools of milky white?

What is this song
that
soars the day
slides down to soak
the night?

*Your eyes are like symphonies, softening the sharp corners of the
earth. Come dear! Your fingertips give rite to every curve. As I arch
toward you, my lips like shadowy petals hunting in the dark for
your liquid flame, you tame me with slow smoldering engulfing
obedience to the Sun. Your fire is on my tongue now, and your
hymn fills me, full-*

diving.

Oh, restless day, be gone!
Leave me to cower in this cold corner with my dark
thoughts.

The sun will soon forget its last setting upon us as we loved
in my mind, alone and tangled.

Tonight, I close my eyes and imagine the taste of your lips
pressed firmly over my mouth,
kisses that end in madness, and tidal waves of bliss.

Tonight, I will dream of you pushing upon me with your
stone body, drenching me in longing looks, your fingers
soaking wet, hands rigid and unyielding.

In another life, another time,
we could have been one
single droplet of water,
always and forever becoming,
becoming,
and becoming
other than
we are
formless, filling me.
Thoughts of you flood me,
holding my body in strange poses, my vagrant tongue in
prayer, back arching,
my tender belly searching for your mouth,
and searching for your mouth,
and searching for your mouth.

I am, in all ways,
always searching
for what the storm of my youth has stolen:
        love,
        is not buried in the sand for us to dig up, wrapped in

careless blankets
       hiding our skin.

It's at the ocean's abyss
with every precious treasure
I have conquered death
to discover.

ashes to desire.

I cannot tell the difference between my hands and those of Pablo
Neruda.
They are the same when pressed together like pines in a forest of
poets,
voices scrambling
for a clearing:

>   to be heard as an original,
>   as one who's traveled the length of a flame,
>   from dying embers to scorching tip,
>   from ashes to desire.

I want to hold a Spanish guitar strum to my breast.
I want to press the language of nature to my lips,
consonants smooth as grapes,
letting it burst on my tongue before I swallow it into my belly and we
become one.

Nature is mine-
>   the curve of hills and rushing plains of white corn,
and forests, and orchards that bear fruit for me.

Our hands touch in this way only-
>   as voices across centuries blow ashes of
>   pagan hymns from one longing life to the next.

My desire is that of nature: to be planted, to blossom, and be picked
>   by God.

eternal traveler.

Sifting through odd ends in the old attic of his soul,
finding love in a time of war,
hiding keepsakes from an enemy.
His body creaks open like an aged cedar chest—

warped & beautiful,
holding inside,
a timepiece, shadow books,
a map of the world,
and a *compass*

to the girl.

At night he has a daydream place,
and his mind becomes an impenetrable fortress.
He is a dark drifter, shape shifter, bending space,
with a safe and secret grip,
burning flame at the tip of a wick,
a   single   candle
flickering free,
         fervent
         pharos

for the girl
to see.

vault of the girl.

Her skin is a watercolor daydream,
swirling sky,
with gothic eyes.
She is a haunting host,
hunting raven circling overhead.
She is the only wetness in this entire desert.

I am almost there,
to his tomb-
one with the stone rolled away.
I know the angel will say, "He is no longer here."

I am making the journey anyway.
I have to see the emptiness for myself.

Maybe he'll be down in a dark cavern cove,
remnants of resurrection on a dusty dirt road.
Maybe I'll see him at the city gates,
collecting offerings,
saving the holy things.

Will he take back his rib from my arch?
Will he say that he put it in the wrong woman?

clear skies.

Driving away from my childhood home last night,

I thought about your eyes.
Could my whole body collapse under your gaze?

Are my hands gripping this wheel in the dark, or are your hands
gripping mine?

I feel as if we have each other in some eternal, ethereal grip,
where time stands still and my mouth melts into yours like a dying
star.

How does your love wreck me and save me from the wreckage all at
once,
bid me to come, and push me aside in the same gesture?

It's clear skies
from here to death-
where my last breath is calling out your name as you press the weight
of your entire world upon me.

process of stars.

My heart hangs lowly in my chest like a dying star,
a red giant,
cooling
and expanding.
Every night I pray it will explode,
that my body will collapse in on itself,
sucking my soul into a black oblivion.

I am told my ending will be the most violent,
that I will be consumed in a fiery explosion
if I continue this trajectory.

As I lay here
in a dark room,
a vastness of space,
I imagine your fingers running through my hair,
your warmth moving over me,
your body—a nuclear force protecting me from myself.

My pale core whimpers.

You clutch me with your fists of iron and nickel,
with your golden ring,
and settle this stellar affliction inside me.

Without you
I am trapped in this process
of sad dreams,
a slow aching, hungry starburst that could swallow a planet
whole,
leaving me nothing but a tiny white light, faint and
flickering.

Your arms are the only thing holding my particles and
plasma together.
Your embrace-
        the only proof that I was ever loved.

to the rhythm of a war drum.

Do your words scare you?
Do your thoughts ever terrify-
                    terrify but never kill?
They beat you back into a caged sleep,
where the aching beast is just beneath,
and you pray for a death that never comes,
drum of your heart piercing the night like a war cry.

All musing and reverie broken by a sick, twisted combat in bed,
your only cavalry:
                    visions in your head
                        of the bright girl!
But a towering darkness builds inside your chest,
that monster you try so desperately to conceal
through excessive dreaming, emotional awol,
shoulders of sad, sloping stone,
belly of warm milk.

Nothing fills like the form of her moving through a room,
your eyes held captive by her shape, the soft, graceful aim of her
gaze.
She is a Nightingale—
            one longing look from her could heal your battle torn body.
            One hymn of her voice could carry you home.

But your words to her will not come,
and the drum ceases its rapid reprise
for a faint, but never fatal cry:

                "Oh, but for one touch of the girl,
                    at long last
                    I could die."

cleverly stamped in red wax.

I remember when your poetry branded my pages
in hot blood-soaked strokes, spurting like warm
red ink in pools at my feet. I wanted to burn
 there with you, gathering my strength from The
Son.

Glory letters, free of fragments, danced
dove-like amidst the flames. I wanted to be your
words, to whip with them in wind and smoke,
sweat with them in chanting huddles, painting
faces and cave dens with curious figures and
scriptures, passing on metaphors like war
tokens.

I was sure you would spend your remaining
years levitating cathedrals and color-wheeling
crucifixes, soaking the streets with Rilke and
Chopin. Over the crowded cities, traffic jams,
and chain-linked hearts of huddled masses, from
strained eyes to cracked lips, your songs would
rain, without pause for pity.

But then, you sent me a card about death.

Death was in the shape of the envelope, the
placement of the stamp in the right-hand corner,
the dried saliva on the folded seal, the wild,
careless cursive parading across soft parchment
like a sad funeral invitation: a caravan of coffins,
white flags, and crooked brows. I saw your
sorry, crumpled face with a smudge of tears,

moistened ink

crinkling the page, foreshadowing of the letter to
come.

I tore you open, sinking my teeth into my
bottom lip, deeper with each word. Where was
the poet who once flooded over bathtubs,
shouting *"why do we crucify ourselves?"* above
the rumble of road construction, and the
redemption of dead widows? You saw through
every optical illusion, every vaginal riddle,
every priest's skirt, every play on words. You
flew over the minds of scholars, landing
lotus-like on their conundrum of furrowed
brows, conjuring pagan secrets you would only
reveal to me in a creaky basement, under the
comfort of an afghan of stars.

I remember.

I loved the portrait of young Mary by your
bedside. I can see her staring into your
constellation-creased face, beyond your event
horizon where no man or God has pressed a
footprint, shed a skin cell, or penetrated a light
beam. This is where your words to me flowed
from: the unscathed space of mysterious
blackness of which I dreamt,

the scrying mirror

from which I saw my own worth.

ever so.

…rustling where no hands can feel,
no wind,
no forgetting.
Her back sloped like white hills,
towing the line of a horizon forever,
pulling away forever.
Following powerlines
into the desert until they disappeared,
she was blown as earth,
worn by
the soft savagery of womanhood,
where the sun eats the moon,
and locusts prepare a place of fire.

Some day-
while bandaging her own wound,
she will bend to be stung by a scorpion crossing her path,
welcoming it with both hands.
If It dies that night in a stream of blood on her belly,
like an insect murdered on a wet rose,
she will know
the slowest death is from self contained violence.
Wind ever so gently pushes dried bones
into a pool of quicksand,
where no man can claim them.

give everything.

I am no promise of spring,

no story of womanhood ending in an old train
rolling toward "*I love you*" in the distance.

I am a memory of something,

a deep sleep overcoming

in the crushing night,

where I am a slave to potions and prayer books.

A bedtime story would be a dream.

Nightmaress are dreams too,

during waking hours when I can't feel my blood
anymore

and it hurts to breathe.

> I would beg for any ease of this blade to cut the
> hope from my chest,
>
> pieces falling to the floor like a storyboard
> writing me into your death.
>
> I'm in my old nightgown now,
>
> with the shades drawn
>
> wondering
>
> if there's a way to make you proud of me
> anymore,

any fortune of comfort you could pull from my
throat,

anything more than these ashes to hold.

here comes the girl.

Her hair is music,
strands of notes
chords,
of hymns,
color of a sunset prayer.
She is a softness of a simpler time when old men, told old
tales in song, in verse,
in waves.
Words have a way with her,
                    if you listen closely.
                    Hold her closely.
                    Bury your face into her.
Breathe in her sound.

                The wind is beating her hair now,
                like a cello bow,
                deep souls twisting to
                a sunkissed crescendo.
                Or is it a slow
                autumn ballad to dance your fingers
                through?
                Push her down and watch her hair roll
                across the ground like a blanket of amber.

Lay with her,
tangled in a braid,
smoke sweetgrass,
from a delicate flame.

elixir.

My elixir is a dark daydream,
shadowy figure in a stolen cloak,
set to blow through me.
> Everything I've ever been
> comes back to this pen.

I am callous from pressing so hard.

My elixir is a warm liquid,
bottled in the background,

> daring me to turn around,
> and drink my entire bloodline down.

compass.

The curtains are panting now
and close themselves.

I breathe into my fists.

Every candle burns down to nothing.

The gray corners of my room take their evil
aim, and map out my body for the night to
claim.

My soul,
desperate as a compass,
wind rose quivering to a point-

where I break against your old, stone chest,
arms aching like sad arrows
trapped by one * infinite * movement.

I long to be lost,
for no bloodline,

for endless storms to crash outside my window,
and make me tremble.
I fear my destiny, immortality,
and the dream
where I die in real life.

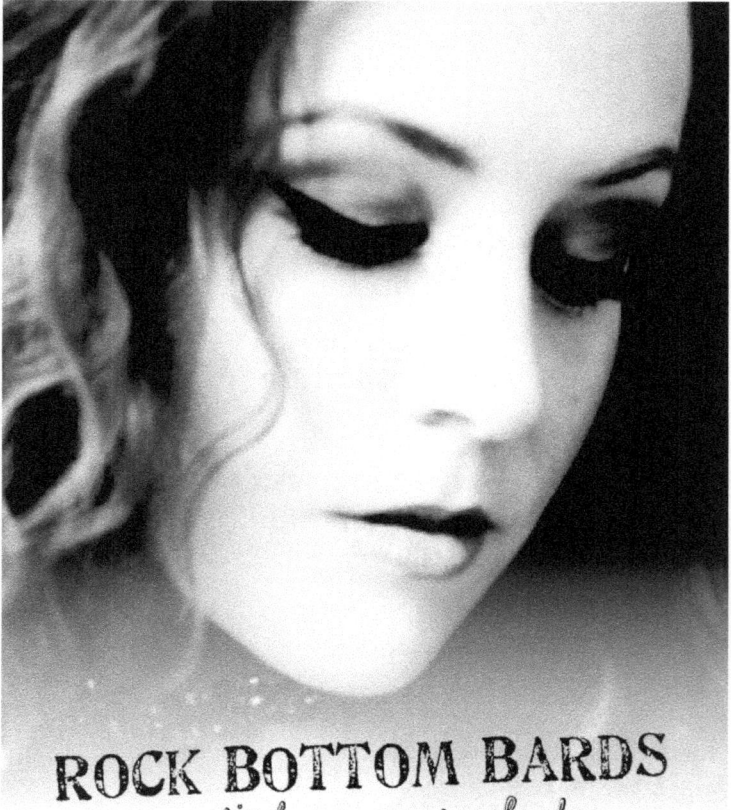

ROCK BOTTOM BARDS
find us on facebook

est. 2025 angiebrownartistry

Angela Brown is a poet and published author from the Detroit area. She earned a Master of Arts in Performance Studies from Eastern Michigan University. She has an extensive background in public speaking, and Ethnographical/Auto-ethnographical Performance. Angela has published poetry in Eastern Michigan University's *Cellar Roots Literary Magazine;* and is a featured poet in UK's Wheelsong Books *Invisible Poets* anthology collection 6. She has published articles in *The Metro Times, Natural Awakenings,* and *The Body, Mind, & Spirit Guide* Detroit area publications. In her spare time, she enjoys reading nonfiction, writing, and sharing with other poets on social media. She is also a proud member of the Crohn's & Colitis Foundation of America, Alcoholics Anonymous, VegMichigan, and the EMU CTA Alumni Group. For more artist info, join her group Rock Bottom Bards on Facebook and Instagram!

www.ingramcontent.com/pod-product-compliance
Lightning Source LLC
Chambersburg PA
CBHW022058080426
42734CB00009B/1396